Chartered Banker

PRACTICE & REVISION KIT
Retail Banking

In this 2014/15 edition
- A **user-friendly format** for easy navigation
- **Updated** on recent developments
- **Question practice on each chapter** to test knowledge retention
- **Exam-standard** mock examinations

Chartered Banker
Leading financial professionalism

Published July 2014

ISBN 978 1 4727 0506 8

British Library Cataloguing-in-Publication Data
A catalogue record for this book
is available from the British Library

Published by

BPP Learning Media Ltd
BPP House, Aldine Place
London W12 8AA

www.bpp.com/learningmedia

Printed in United Kingdom by Ricoh UK Limited
Unit 2,
Wells Place,
Mertsham,
RH1 3LG

Your learning materials, published by BPP Learning Media Ltd, are printed on paper obtained from traceable sustainable sources.

© BPP Learning Media Ltd 2014

All our rights reserved. No part of this publication may be reproduced, stored in a retrieval system or transmitted, in any form or by any means, electronic, mechanical, photocopying, recording or otherwise, without the prior written permission of the Chartered Banker Institute. The descriptions, examples and calculations shown in this publication are for educational purposes only. No liability can be accepted by the Chartered Banker Institute for their use in any circumstances connected with actual trading activity or otherwise. Readers should seek specific advice for specific situations.

CONTENTS

	Page	
	Questions	**Answers**

Question Bank
Chapter 1 – Retail banking	3	27
Chapter 2 – A Client Centred Approach	7	29
Chapter 3 – Distribution Channels and the Impact of Technology	11	31
Chapter 4 – People, Processes and Risk	15	33
Chapter 5 – Leadership and Management	19	35
Chapter 6 – Regulation	23	37

Practice Examinations
Practice Examination 1	39	43
Practice Examination 2	47	51
Practice Examination 3	55	59

QUESTION BANK

Chapter 1 – Retail Banking

1 **Which of the following best describes the fundamental purpose of a bank?**
A   An organisation which lends money
B   An organisation which takes savings
C   An organisation which takes deposits and lends them to those who need funds
D   An organisation which takes savings and lends them to people who need funds

2 **Which of the following terms is used to describe the purpose of a bank?**
A   A provider of financial services
B   A money shop
C   A financial intermediary
D   All of the above

3 **Which of the following best describes the two main types of bank?**
A   Retail and Investment, sometimes known as a merchant bank
B   Retail banks and Building Societies
C   Building Societies and Friendly Societies
D   Credit Unions and Building Societies

4 **What is the primary success criterion of a retail bank?**
A   The making of profit
B   The avoidance of loss
C   The ability to lend money
D   The ability to repay deposits on time

5 **What is the main reason for the intense competition between retail banks?**
A   Customer loyalty to their own bank
B   Because their services are all very similar
C   Because no one trusts any of them any more
D   Because they are all keen to lend only to really safe propositions

6 **A bank, or all banks, could be much more competitive in attracting deposits by a much more dynamic use of interest rates offered to depositors, yet they do not appear to use this as a marketing tool. Why?**
A   Because they cant afford to
B   Because if one did, the others would follow
C   Because the banks operate an interest rate cartel
D   Because they are in a market where they have to buy in funds and sell them at realistic rates

7   **Why were the Country Bankers Act 1826 and the Bank Charter Act 1833 so important to the development of UK banking?**
    A   They were the first pieces of regulation applied to banks in the UK
    B   They created an early form of protection for bank customers
    C   They broke the monopoly of retail banking previously enjoyed by the Bank of England
    D   They permitted anyone to issue bank notes

8   **The period of stability after the First World War was changed by a number of mergers of retail banks in the 1960s. What did this achieve and why was it permitted by the authorities?**
    A   It strengthened bank balance sheets and thus gave greater lending capacity
    B   It created cost savings through economies of scale
    C   It made more funds available for investment in the emerging new technologies that the banks had to consider at the time
    D   All of the above

9   **Which of the following are likely to be characteristics of retail banking in the next decade or so?**
    A   Intense competition leading to mergers and ever larger banks
    B   The splitting up of the large retail banks into community-owned organisations
    C   The concentration by retail banks on the provision of basic deposit taking and lending to sound propositions
    D   The involvement of the banks with ever more complex services, products and investment vehicles

10 **What makes a retail bank profitable?**
    A   The ability not to advertise its lending rates so that it can charge what it wants and thus borrowing customers are at its mercy
    B   Paying very small rates of interest and charging very high rates of interest
    C   Striking a balance between the amounts paid to depositors so as to attract enough funds to lend and the amounts charged to borrowers so as to create more income than is paid to the depositors
    D   All of the above

11 **Why is the asset structure of a bank a compromise between the desire for profit and the need for liquidity?**
    A   Because if a bank has too much liquidity it will not have lent enough and vice versa
    B   Because profit primarily comes from lending interest income and if there is too much liquidity then there is not enough lent out
    C   Because whilst it is safer to retain high liquidity as lots of cash this will be dead money that produces no income to pay the depositors interest
    D   All of the above

12 **What is the main driver of the creation of profit by a bank?**
   A   Greed
   B   A danger that if profits are perceived to be too low, a competitor may make a takeover bid
   C   A need for cash
   D   All of the above

13 **How does a retail bank contribute to the world economy?**
   A   By making profits it makes a contribution to the growth of the economy
   B   By providing credit it enables businesses and individuals to contribute to the world economy
   C   By creating money it makes more available to the world economy
   D   All of the above

14 **How does the creation of profit by a bank help the world economy?**
   A   Banks distribute some profits as dividends and this makes money available for consumption and investment by shareholders
   B   Banks pay taxes on their profits to governments, which assists the economy
   C   Profits can be used by banks as sources of funding which makes more credit available and thus assists the economy
   D   All of the above

15 **Why is it that if a bank has too much money tied up in lending its future may be in danger?**
   A   Because it might have lent cash that could be demanded by depositors
   B   Because it might have over-lent to a specific industrial sector and if there are problems in that sector it might take serious bad debts
   C   Because it will prevent it lending to other customers who might give a faster and safer return
   D   All of the above

Chapter 2 – A Client Centred Approach

1 **Which of the following is characteristic of a customer centred approach?**
   A   An organisation which is concerned with operational imperatives but always tries to have the highest possible service levels
   B   An organisation which tries to do what customers ask promptly and with excellent service levels
   C   An organisation which tries to do what customers ask and tries to draw to customers attention other things which it thinks customers might need
   D   An organisation which avoids selling beyond what the customer asks for to avoid any risks of mis-selling

2 **There is a real danger to adopting a customer centred approach which outweighs all other negatives that might arise from it. Which of the following is this?**
   A   That over-enthusiastic staff might sell customers something that they neither need nor want
   B   That customers might not want to be bothered by staff who could be seen to be overly fussy and sales orientated
   C   That the costs of being customer centred might outweigh the financial and other advantages
   D   All of the above

3 **Which of the following best encapsulates the spirit of an organisation if it properly adopts a customer centred approach, rather than just paying the term lip service?**
   A   An organisation that does everything a customer wants and more
   B   An organisation that does everything a customer wants and which anticipates needs before the customer does
   C   An organisation which does everything a customer wants, which anticipates needs and does not charge for its services
   D   An organisation which does everything a customer wants, which anticipates needs but which is more expensive than its competitors

4 **Which of the following is the fundamental factor in the delivery of a customer centred approach by any organisation, but particularly a bank?**
   A   Infrastructure
   B   Staff
   C   Organisational culture
   D   Customer loyalty

5 **What is a customer?**
   A   Someone who uses an ATM machine
   B   Someone who asks a bank for advice
   C   Someone who has or intends to have an account
   D   All of the above

6 Which of the following is not one of the duties of a banker to their customers?

A To provide overdraft accommodation if needed
B To pay written orders from the customer if there are funds to meet them
C To always act in good faith and without negligence
D To give reasonable notice of the closure of an account

7 Which of the following is not a duty of a customer to their banker?

A To take care of his cheque book and cards
B To pay charges and fees
C To advise the bank of any forgery of his signature
D To exercise reasonable care in drawing up his written orders and instructions to the bank

8 Which of the following are the rights of a banker against his customer?

A A right to charge reasonable commissions and fees
B A right to interest
C A right to set off accounts and refuse to honour a written order when there are insufficient funds to meet it
D All of the above

9 When might a banker breach the otherwise absolute duty of secrecy that the banker has to customers, in order to avoid an action for breach of contract?

A Compelled to do so by law
B If there is a duty to the public to disclose the information or in the interests of the bank
C With the customers express or implied consent
D All of the above

10 What is set-off?

A The point at which an account legally, can be operated
B The point at which legally the banker-customer relationship starts
C The point at which an overdraft is made available to the customer
D The combining of a credit balance with a debit one, to reduce or repay the latter

11 What is the significance of Claytons case?

A It establishes which debit is extinguished by which credit and vice versa
B It lays down the rules by which a debit balance must be repaid
C It lays down the rules by which cash is paid in for debts
D It permits the bank to decide in the absence of instructions from the customer, which credits will be applied to which debits

12 What is an overdraft?

A A legally binding agreement for the bank to provide funds to a customer
B A negative balance on a current account
C A positive balance on a current account
D A loan

13 What is the difference between a loan and an overdraft?

A A loan is provided under a set of legally binding contractual terms one of which sets out the arrangements for repayment, an overdraft though is repayable on demand
B A loan is for a specific good, an overdraft can be used for anything
C An overdraft is an emergency back stop provided in case of need, a loan is provided for a specific purchase
D An overdraft is repayable at the end of the year, a loan is repayable according to the contract

14 What is the difference between a standing order and a direct debit?

A A standing order is claimed by the beneficiary, a direct debit is paid by the bank of the customer who owes money to the beneficiary
B A direct debit is claimed by the beneficiary or his bank, a standing order is paid by the bank of the customer who owes money to the beneficiary
C A standing order can operate on a savings account, a direct debit can only operate on a current account
D A standing order can operate on a savings account, a direct debit can operation on either a savings or a current account

15 What is the fundamental need of a bank if it is to be able to provide a customer centred approach?

A An excellent and accurate knowledge of the customer
B Good infrastructure to provide information about its customers
C A wide range of products and services
D All of the above

Chapter 3 – Distribution Channels and the Impact of Technology

1. **Which of the following is the main risk to banks in relation to customers using the banks ATMs?**
   A That the customer will lose their card and Personal Identification Number
   B That the customer will be mugged whilst using the machine
   C That the customer will fail to take their cash from the machine
   D That the customer will fail to take their card from the machine

2. **Which of the following is not within the capability of an ATM?**
   A Display and print a balance
   B Transfer money to another account
   C Arrange a mortgage secured loan
   D Pay out cash against an overdraft limit

3. **What is the main risk to the customer of using an automatic pay in machine with a 'quick deposit' envelope?**
   A That they will be mugged whilst using the machine in the banking hall
   B That the bank will lose the deposit and they will have no receipt to prove that it took place
   C That the customer will dispute the amount that they deposited
   D That the customer will write the wrong amount on the envelope

4. **Which of the following statements is correct?**
   A Telephone banking is a form of direct banking
   B Telephone banking is only offered by banks with no branch network
   C Telephone banking is more complex to access than internet banking
   D Telephone banking only uses IT-based systems

5. **What is the difference between an internet bank and a clicks and mortar bank?**
   A There is no difference
   B They can both offer direct services online
   C Traditional banks offer a much more personal service than an internet bank does
   D Traditional banks provide lending facilities, an internet bank does not

6. **A customer accumulates more points in a credit scoring exercise than the minimum required. What does this mean to the bank?**
   A They will be offered a greater amount of credit than they requested
   B That they exceed the minimum risk levels sought for consideration when applying for a loan
   C That they will repay the loan that they have asked for
   D That there is no risk in lending to this customer

7 What is the underlying premise of credit scoring?

A It looks at an applicants past record and makes a decision and/or recommendation based upon that

B It looks at the application and makes a decision based against a range of historical information

C It looks at the banks credit appetite and makes a decision based upon that and the content of the application

D All of the above

8 Which of the following is a real, emergent and developing danger to banks as a result of the many distribution channels now available to the banks?

A That management will not keep up to date with technology

B That technology will become dominant over banking

C That the size and diversity of the operations might creative internal competition for the same business

D That the costs of technology will negate its advantages

9 Cash is a simple means of money transmission which is very cheap to use as it is provided by the state. Why do banks discourage its use?

A It needs a lot of staff to deal with it

B Holding it costs the bank lost interest

C Alternatives to cash are very much cheaper

D All of the above

10 Why do banks dislike cheques do much?

A For the same reasons as they dislike cash

B They do not dislike cheques

C They carry quite a lot of legal commercial risk

D They are difficult to handle

11 Why do customers like cheques?

A They can be made out for any amount

B They can be sent through the post easily and thus avoid transmission costs beyond a stamp

C They are signed and therefore perceived as safe

D All of the above

12 Tactically, how do banks overcome most of the problems that they have with cheques?

A Encouraging on line transactions instead

B Truncation of the payment

C They dont and thus encourage customers not to use them

D By recovering their costs via the delays in the clearing system

13 **What is the paper credit equivalent of a cheque?**

A   A direct debit instruction

B   A standing order instruction

C   A bank giro credit form

D   There is no equivalent

14 **How can technology help to introduce a new customer effectively to the bank?**

A   By providing regular contacts, as necessary using information provided

B   By providing regular contacts with the customer to advise them of all services available

C   By following their behaviour and selling them the products this suggests that they will appreciate

D   All of the above

15 **How can IT help with fulfilling customer needs and wants?**

A   By categorising customers into happy, unhappy and indifferent and reacting accordingly

B   By following their spending habits and reacting accordingly

C   By sending them product information based on what they do not use

D   All of the above

Chapter 4 – People, Processes and Risk

1. **The shift of work from retail branches to processing centres resulted in some serious problems for the banks and their customers which previously simply had not happened. Which of the following was the major problem?**
   A A lack of personal service
   B Increased costs
   C Increased time to process customer requests
   D Increased errors

2. **As centralised processing took place there was an increase in frustration to customers. What was the major reason for this?**
   A If errors took place, the banks tended to pass the blame between the branch and the processing centre
   B Low morale
   C Low pay at the processing centres
   D All of the above

3. **What is the nature of a service level agreement?**
   A An internal contract between two or more parts of an organisation
   B A promise by a bank to provide a certain level of service to its customers
   C A promise by any organisation of a minimum level of service
   D The agreement of two providers that the service they provide to a third party will be of a minimum level

4. **Why are service level agreements important when they never used to exist?**
   A Because service is provided to the external customer by a combination of parts of an organisation. Each needs to rely upon a minimum level of service from the other
   B Because costs need to be contained
   C Because so many errors take place when central processing is used
   D All of the above

5. **What is the major advantage of a Service Level Agreement?**
   A It shows everyone what to expect and what to promise
   B It shows the customer what to expect and how much it will cost
   C It shows who will do what, when and how
   D It allows all aspects of service provided to and by internal customers to be established in a calm environment, rather than as a response to a crisis

6. **Which of the following situations would be ideally situated for a bank to outsource?**
   A The provision of an occasional specialist service
   B The provision of a regular but non-core activity
   C The provision of an expensive non-core activity
   D All of the above

7   **What is the purpose of a third party policy?**
    A   To ensure consistency
    B   To save time
    C   To save money
    D   To keep head count down

8   **Your study text describes risk as the possibility of loss, injury, disadvantage or destruction. Which of the following also describe risk?**
    A   A danger
    B   Something happening that is unexpected
    C   A loss of money
    D   A loss of anything that you wished to keep

9   **What is the process of managing risk?**
    A   Recognising a potential risk and putting something in the plan to cover this eventuality
    B   Ensuring that all possible risks are covered in the plan
    C   Ensuring that all likely or reasonably likely risks are covered in the plan
    D   Ensuring that the plan includes recognising reasonable risks and the steps to be taken to mitigate them

10 **What is credit risk?**
    A   The risk that a banks credit will be impaired
    B   The risk that a banks supply of credit will be cut off
    C   The risk that a loan made by a bank will not be repaid as agreed
    D   The risk that a loan made by a bank will not be repaid

11 **What is market risk?**
    A   A loss due to a shift interest rates
    B   A loss due to a shift in commodity prices or values
    C   A loss due to a shift in exchange rates
    D   All of the above

12 **What is liquidity risk?**
    A   The bank not having enough cash to pay to depositors when they demand repayment
    B   The bank not being able to access liquid funds to lend to new customers
    C   The bank too many notes and coins and losing interest as a result
    D   Customers losing confidence in the bank

13 **What is regulatory risk?**
    A   A risk that regulations will be imposed that will harm the business
    B   A risk that the bank will breach regulatory requirements
    C   A risk that the banks reputation will be damaged by failing to comply with regulatory requirements
    D   All of the above

14   What is operational risk?

   A   A failure of internal processes
   B   The failure of people to do their jobs properly
   C   The failure of a system
   D   All of the above

15   Which of the following represent external risk?

   A   Risks which come from activities which are outside the control of the bank
   B   A change in the tax arrangements to which the bank is subject
   C   The loss of electrical power
   D   All of the above

Chapter 5 – Leadership and Management

1 **What is the span of control?**
   A   The period of time over which a manager manages the organisation
   B   The size of the organisation that someone leads
   C   The number of people for whom a manager or leader is directly responsible
   D   The number of functional areas for which a manager or leader is responsible

2 **What is effective management?**
   A   Management that delivers the objectives which are set for it
   B   Management which keeps costs to a minimum and delivers its objectives
   C   Management which is achieves the most with the least resources
   D   All of the above

3 **What is meant by efficiency?**
   A   Getting the job done as cheaply and/or as fast as possible
   B   It is a measure of how well results are achieved
   C   How well results are achieved from limited resources
   D   It is a measure of the production of results compared to the use of inputs

4 **What is meant by the term effective?**
   A   It is a measure of how accurately the required results were achieved
   B   It is a measure of how efficiently the required results were achieved
   C   It is a measure of accuracy of the team
   D   It is a measure of how quickly the required results were achieved

5 **What is meant by equity in relation to the management of an organisation?**
   A   It is the amount of working capital available to managers
   B   It is the amount of unencumbered assets available to an organisation
   C   It recognises that the need for managers to treat all who work for and receive services from them fairly
   D   It is a reference to the need to treat all staff objectively

6 **How ought management be measured?**
   A   By a combination of measures of its efficiency, effectiveness and equity
   B   By how well it gets the job done
   C   By its success
   D   By all of the above

7 What is the difference between management and leadership?
A There is no difference
B Leadership is about getting things done, management is about doing them
C Management is about getting things done, leadership is about doing them
D Leadership is about getting things done through people

8 What is an organisation?
A It is any business unit or combination of business units
B It is any company military unit or not for profit operation that is trying to achieve something
C It is anything that has more than one person in it
D It is a combination of people with a structure and purpose

9 What does a manager do?
A Uses or creates a structure with people to achieve a purpose
B Manage people
C Communicate and manage resources
D All of the above

10 Which of the following differentiates the role of a manager and a leader?
A They both have to deliver to a purpose
B A leader always has a team, a manager marshals resources
C A leader can lead without being managed but a manager cant manage without being led
D Manager and leaders are in effect the same thing, there is no real difference

11 What is the difference between tactics and strategy?
A There is no difference
B There is a difference but it is not usually discernible; one persons tactics is anothers strategy
C Tactics are how the strategy is delivered; strategy is about why that delivery is needed and its purpose
D Strategy is long term, tactics are about day to day operations

12 What are the likely components of a business strategy for a bank?
A Retail and corporate
B How to make a profit
C Corporate, unit and operational
D How to be effective

13 Is it true to say that strategic management is divorced from operational planning?
A Yes
B No
C Not always
D Impossible to say

14   How might success be measured?
   A   Using hard, realistic, sensible, time limited goals, objectives or targets
   B   By the size of profit made
   C   By the size of the limitation of loss
   D   By how happy customers are

15   Which of the following would you say are the key stakeholders in a bank which therefore in turn need to be satisfied by its performance?
   A   Shareholders and the management
   B   Shareholders, Investors, staff, customers
   C   The government, shareholders and investors
   D   The government and the boar

Chapter 6 – Regulation

1. **Which one of the following is NOT part of the Bank of England?**
   A The Prudential Regulation Authority
   B The Financial Conduct Authority
   C The Financial Policy Committee
   D The Note Issue Department

2. **The detailed rules pertaining to UK financial services regulation are set out in which one of the following?**
   A The Regulators' Handbooks
   B The Financial Services and Markets Act 2000
   C The Regulators' Sourcebooks
   D The Financial Services Act 1986

3. **Responsibility for a firm's compliance with TCF lies with which one of the following?**
   A The Compliance Officer
   B All employees of the firm
   C The regulated sales force
   D The Board of Directors

4. **The main difference between the Banking Conduct of Business Sourcebook and the Banking Code is:**
   A BCOBS makes it easier for customers to complain about their bank
   B Compliance with BCOBS is mandatory, the Banking Code was voluntary
   C BCOBS covers all activities of firms
   D BCOBS lays out specific penalties for non-compliance

5. **Which one of the following organisations is covered by the Lending Code?**
   A A charity with income of £500,000
   B A business employing 12 people
   C A business with a balance sheet value of €3m
   D A business with a turnover of €2.5m

6. **To qualify as a 'regulated mortgage contract' how much of the property must be used for residential purposes, assuming that all other qualification aspects are met?**
   A 25%
   B 30%
   C 40%
   D 50%

7   Which one of the following organisations is responsible for the development of the Basel Accords?
    A   The European Central Bank
    B   The Bank for International Settlements
    C   The European Securities and Markets Authority
    D   The International Monetary Fund

8   Consumer credit in the UK is regulated by:
    A   The Financial Conduct Authority
    B   The Bank of England
    C   The Financial Ombudsman
    D   The Office of Fair Trading

9   The upper limit for lending to be regulated by the Consumer Credit Acts is:
    A   £25,000
    B   £75,000
    C   £150,000
    D   There is no upper limit

10 The final stage of the money laundering process is called:
    A   Layering
    B   Placement
    C   Integration
    D   Absorption

11 Data relating to a person's religion is deemed to be:
    A   Personal data
    B   Restricted data
    C   Confidential data
    D   Sensitive data

ANSWER BANK

RETAIL BANKING: ANSWER BANK

Chapter 1 – Retail Banking

1 **C** A bank takes deposits, not always savings, from those with an excess of cash and lends these to those who are short of cash.

2 **C** A bank is a financial intermediary. It takes money from one group of customers which it then owes to them and lends it to another, which owes it to the bank.

3 **A** The primary and secondary banks are known as retail and investment banks. The latter are sometimes referred to as merchant banks.

4 **D** Banks must retain the confidence of their customers. There are two types of customers who sometimes are the same person, depositors and borrowers. Banks' funds though come in the main from having enough depositors cash to make loans and then to be able to repay the depositors' funds when they are due, or on demand according to the agreement. If a bank is not able to do this, then the public will lose confidence in it and a run on the bank is almost certain to happen. This is when a very large number of customers demand their money back all at once, to the point where the bank does not have enough cash left to repay them all, as it only retains a small proportion of the deposited funds as cash, the remainder having been lent to borrowing customers. The main success criteria of a bank on a day to day basis, must be its ability to repay depositors when due.

5 **B** Most of the retail banks provide the same services 'packaged' under different names. The public have a huge choice as to which bank to use, as all the services work more or less just as well as the others. Therefore there is massive competition between the large number of organisations involved.

6 **D** If banks offered very high interest rates to depositors then they would have to charge higher rates to borrowers. Although the high rates would attract depositors only those who were desperate or relatively desperate would borrow at the essential higher rates that would have to be charged. Thus, there would be fewer or no safe borrowers and the only way that the bank could make its money on the difference between what it charges and pays would be by taking on lots of poor lending, a high proportion of which would be likely to default. This would put the deposits in danger. This situation would be known to many depositors from the outset and might damage confidence, and actually reduce the amount deposited.

7 **C** They created the legal opportunity for banks other than the Bank of England to provide retail banking first outside, then within, London.

8 **D** All of these factors resulted from and were the reasons why these mergers took place.

9 **C** The future is hard to predict, but it is more than likely that banks will regardless of size, concentrate on more tradition retail functions and lending to sound propositions, rather than indulging in some of the more esoteric activities and lending in which they were involved in the years up to 2007 if they are to remain profitable and safe.

10 **C** A cynic might say that the answer is D. In fact, market forces will always ensure that a bank has to pay realistic rates to depositors if it is to maintain its flow of funds so that it can lend and to lend, it will have to charge competitive rates compared to the others in the lending market. Profit comes from the difference between the two.

11	D	A B and C are all correct and actually say the same thing in different ways. If there is too much cash (liquidity) then there will be a lot of dead money that could be lent out, but if there is not enough cash, then there will be too much lent out and a danger that although a good income is likely, depositors might not be able to be paid out when due. Banking is therefore a constant balancing act between a need to make profits and a need to retain liquidity.
12	B	Banks need to make profit for a variety of reasons, but the main competitive force is to keep the shareholders happy with dividends and capital growth. If they are not happy, there is a danger that they might sell to a competitor and a takeover happen; in turn this would threaten the management's position.
13	D	All options contribute to the world economy.
14	D	All options are correct.
15	D	All options are true.

Chapter 2 – A Client Centred Approach

1	C	A customer centred organisation will always try to do not only what the customer knows he wants, but also to try to anticipate demands, but without selling him things he does not need.
2	A	There is a real danger that without top rate training staff might go too far and do more damage than good by providing services to a customer that go beyond their needs or wants. The PPI scandal being a good example of this.
3	B	A customer centred approach should deliver what the customer asks for (which includes promptness and accuracy) or if not, is able to explain fully why not, and which is able to look forward to address the customers' real, genuine needs and potential ones, which they may not presently be aware of.
4	B	Customer service is delivered by staff, even if it is IT based, because real people have to design it and make it happen in the first place. It therefore follows that staff are the foundation of a customer centred approach in banking.
5	C	All legal precedents point towards a customer being someone who has, or who intends to open an account.
6	A	A bank is under no legal, moral or commercial duty automatically to provide an overdraft. The other alternatives are all part of the banker's duty to his customer under the Joachimson rules.
7	A	Remarkably, there is no legal onus on a customer to take care of his cheque book and cards. There is however a requirement that the customer advises the bank of any actual or suspected forgery and that they will take reasonable care when drawing up his written instructions. This, it has been pointed out on more than one occasion, means that although a customer must advise the bank if they suspects that a forgery may have taken place, they can happily and without fear walk down the street strewing their cheques to the four winds, so long as they are not aware of anyone picking them up to mis-use them, in which case the customer would have to report a potential forgery to the bank.
8	D	All four rights are those which accrue to a banker as a result of the contract with the customer.
9	D	All of the alternatives are examples of when a bank may breach its duty of secrecy.
10	D	'Set-off' is precisely what it says. It is the off-setting of a credit balance in the name and ownership of a customer (said to be in the same right) with a debit balance under precisely the same ownership and control. The purpose is to reduce or remove the debit balance.
11	A	It sets of the dictum that the first credit in extinguishes the first debit out and vice versa.
12	B	An overdraft is facilitated by a current account which carries a negative balance.
13	A	Both must be repaid, but a loan always has an agreement which sets out the repayment terms. As long as these are kept, the loan is not in default and the bank cannot demand repayment forthwith. An overdraft though, whatever other terms may apply, is always repayable on demand, regardless of its history.

14   **A**   A direct debit is claimed, a standing order is paid.

15   **A**   The basic thing that a bank needs to provide a customer centred approach is that it must know about each customer and their needs, so that these can be delivered against.

Chapter 3 – Distribution Channels and the Impact of Technology

1	**A**	Banks generally have to rely on the customers not losing both card and PIN. If they do, the bank may have to stand, and often does stand, any consequent loss.
2	**C**	ATMs can not arrange mortgaged backed loans.
3	**B**	The customer cannot be given a receipt other than at best, for the deposit of the envelope. Therefore it is quite possible that the system could 'lose' the envelope and/or deposit, leaving the customer with no proof that they had tried to undertake the transaction.
4	**A**	Telephone banking is one form of direct banking. Both direct and telephone banking can offer telephone banking services and there is no difference in the complexity of accessing telephone and internet banking.
5	**B**	They both provide a range of core facilities which are the same – with the traditional bank able to offer service son the High Street and via the internet.
6	**B**	By exceeding the credit scoring minimum figure, all that is meant is that the applicant meets the minimum risk level for the application. It does not necessarily mean that the loan will be repaid. There will still be a risk to the bank that the customer will not be able to repay the loan, but the level of risk is deemed to be within the bank's risk appetite.
7	**D**	Credit scoring is a complex operation which takes into account the customer, their personal circumstances and their borrowing record, the record of similar customers and the bank's own wish to lend in the circumstances of the application.
8	**C**	The others can be managed, but there is a real danger that with many types of delivery channel, one part of the bank might start inadvertently to compete with others.
9	**C**	Although at first sight cash is cost free, and it is more or less to the customer/user, for those charged with its movement and storage, it is very expensive in itself and hugely so compared to the alternatives.
10	**A**	Banks dislike cheques almost as much as cash for the same reasons. They are in comparison to the alternatives bulky to handle, expensive to move about and require lots of people and equipment to deal with them.
11	**D**	Customers like cheques for all of these reasons.
12	**B**	The main way they avoid the immediate difficulties is by a process called truncation which avoids the banks passing large numbers of pieces of paper between each other. A C and D are actually wrong as such, it is just that truncation in the short term avoids most of the problems that arise through the use of cheques. Strategically to get people to use them less, the banks use the techniques in A C and D to discourage their use in the long term.
13	**C**	A bank giro credit transfer money from one person to another so it is, in effect, like a cheque but to transfer a credit, rather than being a written instruction to transfer funds.

14   **A**   IT can carefully and subtly (as well as morally) provide a means by which the bank can gently introduce itself and its services to the new customer, without making them feel that they are being sold everything that they may (or may not) want or need.

15   **A**   The fundamental way that IT can help is first of all to try to identify whether they are happy with the bank, indifferent to it or unhappy and then to provide support to them which fits that category, as designed by the bank.

Chapter 4 – People, Processes and Risk

1   **C**   The initial problem faced was increased time to process customer requests due to the distances involved.

2   **A**   Generally speaking, the move to such centres created an opportunity for delays and errors to be blamed by those dealing with customers on others in the chain that undertook the work, usually the processing centre. This caused great frustration to customers who simply wanted their requirements meeting by whatever means. They were not interested in why things did not happen, nor on blaming certain places or individuals, they just wanted their instructions carryied out promptly and accurately.

3   **A**   A form of non-legally binding contract (an agreement) as to the minimum levels of service that one part of an organisation will provide to another.

4   **A**   The combining of parts of a bank to provide a service to an external customer requires them all to work to provide internal service to a predictable minimal level. Otherwise promises made by one part of the organisation to the external customer might not be met.

5   **D**   SLAs are agreed outside the day to day operating environment. This means that they can be arrived at in a measured and sensible way. They do not require a knee jerk response to a crisis.

6   **D**   Any service which is non-core (and some which are) can be outsourced.

7   **A**   Such a policy is used primarily to ensure that decisions to outsource are taken on a consistent basis and that the consequent dealings with third parties are similarly consistent and to a common template.

8   **B**   Risk is simply something happening that is not in the plan for the event, project or process. Thus risk can be very small (it might rain, but you have a roof) or it might be catastrophic (it might pour down, your roof leaks and the business sinks). But it is, in the main, something happening that was not in the plan.

9   **D**   You can only manage so much risk and have to be realistic about it. But its management is recognising what you can manage and how it will be managed and what levels of risk are acceptable.

10   **C**   Credit risk the risk that a loan, once made, will not be repaid according to the agreement with the borrower.

11   **D**   Any loss or impairment to a bank's business due to changes in the financial markets is a market risk.

12   **A**   Liquidity risk refers to the bank being able to have adequate funds to pay out (usually in cash) its depositors when they demand repayment.

13   **C**   The bank's reputation is at risk if it breaches current regulations.

14   **D**   Operational risk is any risk that arises as a result of process, system or people failures to do what they are supposed to do properly, as well as the risks arising from external events.

15   **D**   An external risk is any risk which is due to the failure of outside circumstances to occur as expected or predicted.

Chapter 5 – Leadership and Management

1   **C**   The span of control refers to the number of direct reports any one person is responsible for. The terms comes from General Sir Ian Hamilton in his seminal work on the management and organisation of the British Army 'The Soul and Body of an Army'.

2   **A**   Effective in terms of management can only refer to a management which does what it is there to do. This usually means delivering to the objectives which it sets for itself or which are set for it. These usually include issues such as resource management in addition to the principle purpose of the organisation or sub-organisation that is being managed.

3   **D**   To be efficient is to produce as much as possible from as little as possible.

4   **A**   It is a measure of how accurately the required results were achieved. On its own, other measures of success to do enter into the equation which is why success can only be measured in terms of efficiency, effectiveness.

5   **C**   Managers must act with equity towards all who work for them and who are their customers or who are affected by their actions. Otherwise trust from the team, trust from the customers and trust from the wider community towards the organisation will break down, sometimes with incalculable consequences as has been seen in the banking industry in the UK. The LIBOR scandal reported in 2012 is a classic example of this.

6   **A**   This is the only precise measure.

7   **D**   As the text suggests and Eisenhower wrote, leadership is about getting someone to do something that you want doing because he wants (for whatever reason) to do it.

8   **D**   There is a difference between a group of people and an organisation. An organisation has at the least a purpose and hopefully a structure that may or may not enable it to achieve that purpose.

9   **A**   A manager uses an organisation to deliver a purpose.

10   **C**   No-one managed Churchill, but he had plenty of people (who were also leaders) in his span of control who could not have managed without his leadership. The same applies at levels of business and organisational control, although the differences might not, in fact probably will not, be so marked or discernible.

11   **C**   Strategy is concerned with where the organisation is going or why it going there or both, tactics are about how it gets there. Nelson laid down his purpose as being about identifying and how to and then destroying as many French and Spanish ships as possible, that was tactical. His manager, the First Lord of the Admiralty, Lord Barham's job was to direct the overall naval war and prevent a French invasion of the UK, which was strategy.

12   **C**   A bank is usually divided in to the overall corporate organisation, its component business units and some form of operational purpose. Therefore an overall strategy which will be complex is required for each of these areas. It is almost certain that in creating this strategy, there will be elements of tactical planning incorporated in the strategic plan.

13   **B**   The management of strategy cannot possibly be divorced from operation planning. You cannot make strategic plans for something which is operationally impossible. You can though set testing targets for the operational managers who will be required to deliver the strategic objectives.

14   **A**   Success can and should be measured across purpose, however it is termed. It can only be measured if the metrics used to achieve that measure are realistic & sensible (i.e. they can be achieved although that may be hard to do), they need to be hard (i.e. specific) and need to have a time upon them by when they will be measured.

15   **B**   The main groups with interest in the performance of a bank are shareholders and investors, the staff at all levels and customers.

Chapter 6 – Regulation

1	B	The FCA is not part of the Bank of England, the other options are all sections of the bank.
2	C	The detailed rules are laid down in the Sourcebooks. The Handbooks lay out a framework.
3	D	Whilst many employers may deliver TCF, responsibility for compliance lies with the Board.
4	B	Firms must comply with the requirements of BCOBS, whereas the Banking Code was a voluntary Code.
5	A	As the requirements are a business with turnover or balance sheet value of under €2m, employing less than 10 people, or a charity with total income under £1m.
6	C	At least 40% of the property must be used for residential purposes to be deemed a regulated mortgage contract.
7	B	It is the Bank for International Settlement (BIS) that develops the Basel Accords.
8	D	The Office of Fair Trading (OFT) regulates consumer credit and grants consumer credit licenses.
9	D	The 2006 Act removed the previous ceiling of £25,000 so there is no upper limit unless the borrower has grounds to opt out and has acted on these.
10	C	Integration is the final stage, where funds are converted to look as though they are legitimate.
11	D	Such information is deemed to be sensitive data under the terms of the Data Protection Act.

PRACTICE EXAMINATION 1

PRACTICE EXAM 1: QUESTIONS

Question 1

Required

(a) Describe the differences between a retail and a wholesale bank. **(8 marks)**

(b) Discuss why it is important that one retail bank is seen as being different from a competitor. **(12 marks)**

(c) Bank interest rates are usually very similar. Consider why this is the case. **(10 marks)**

(TOTAL 30 MARKS)

Question 2

Required

What are the rights and duties of

(a) A customer of a bank, and

(a) A bank with regard to its customer? **(TOTAL 20 MARKS)**

Question 3

Required

Explain why Clayton's claim was not accepted and why it is of such importance to a banker.

(TOTAL 15 MARKS)

Question 4

Required

(a) Consider why most retail banks use several different channels. Illustrate your answer with examples. **(10 marks)**

(b) Discuss the role of people in providing some methods of delivery for bank services and why face-to-face contact can be very important in some circumstances but less so in others. Illustrate your answer with examples.

(10 marks)

(TOTAL 20 MARKS)

Question 5

Required

Explain what is meant by the term organisation. **(TOTAL 15 MARKS)**

PRACTICE EXAM 1: ANSWERS

Answer 1

(a) Describe the differences between a retail and a wholesale bank. **(8 marks)**

Your answer should have included the following points.

- Generally retail banks have large branch networks and are willing to deal in sums of money both large and small.
- Wholesale banks usually do not have branch or other 'distribution' networks and usually only deal in large sums of money.
- Retail banks tend to be those which operate the money transfer system.
- Wholesale banks do not usually involve themselves in money transfer systems, other than as users.

(b) Discuss why it is important that one retail bank is seen as being different from a competitor.

Your answer should have included the following points. **(12 marks)**

- They are all seen as providing more or less the same services.
- Which means that in the eyes of the public, their customers, there is little to choose between them.
- The banks need many customers to survive as they need their cash to remain liquid and provide funds to lend.
- There is therefore intense commercial and competitive pressure to obtain business.
- But if there is no public perception of difference, there is no reason why customers should choose one bank rather than another.
- Unless each bank is able to show why a customer should go to it rather than any of its competitors it is in danger of either losing customers or not having enough.
- Which could lead to their failure due to lack of cash.

(c) Bank interest rates are usually very similar. Consider why this is the case. **(10 marks)**

Your answer should have included the following points.

- Banks have to pay interest to attract customers with deposits.
- They also have to charge interest to borrowers.
- The difference is their profit.
- As they all do the same thing and are (more or less) in competition for the same business.
- Their rates have to be competitive with each other.
- Therefore, there is almost bound to be very little difference between the rates offered for similar services.
- Also the banks all look to the Money Market for much of their cash which they have to borrow.
- LIBOR is the governing rate there which is common across all banks so they are starting from a standard base.
- Unless the market sees a particular bank as being much less risky than its competitors, the rates charged are going to be similar.

(TOTAL 30 MARKS)

RETAIL BANKING

Answer 2

What are the rights and duties of

(a) A customer of a bank, and

(a) A bank with regard to its customer? **(TOTAL 20 MARKS)**

Your answer should include the following points.

- Rights and Duties arise from the contract between bank and customer
- Defined by common law. Cases:
    - Foley v Hill (1848) relationship is one of a debtor and creditor
    - Great Western Railway v London & County Banking Co. (1921) someone is not a customer unless they have an account
    - Taxation Commissioners v English Scottish & Australian Bank (1920) someone becomes a customer when they open an account
    - Woods v Martins Bank (1959) someone can be a customer before they have an account if the intention is to open one
    - Joachimson v Swiss Bank Corporation (1921) sets out duties and rights:

Bankers duties are:

- Receive and collect money for the account
- Provided correctly drawn and there is enough money, to pay customer's written instructions
- If payment of a cheque is refused, to do this in good faith and without negligence
- To maintain secretary of the customer's affairs
- To advise the customer of suspected fraud
- To give reasonable notice of closure of the account

Customer's duties are:

- To use reasonable care when drawing up written instructions
- To advise the bank when forgery is suspected
- To pay charges

Bank's rights are:

- To charge reasonable fees for services
- To charge interest for borrowing
- To set off credit against debit balances
- To return unpaid any cheques which will create an unauthorised debit balance

Customer's rights are:

- Non are specified but it does not seem unreasonable for the customer to expect the bank to abide by his duties

PRACTICE EXAM 1: ANSWERS

Answer 3

Explain why Clayton's claim was not accepted and why it is of such importance to a banker.

(TOTAL 15 MARKS)

Your answer should have included the following points.

- Case is actually Devaynes v Noble (1816).
- Involved a bank partnership which went into insolvency.
- Clayton was a customer who between a partner's death and the bank's insolvency withdrew more than his balance at the time of the death.
- He claimed from the estate of the partner the balance of his account as at the date of death.
- But also over that period paid in more than that sum.
- Judge said that the balance as at the date of death was not the same balance at the date of insolvency.
- Because the money had been withdrawn and replaced by new deposits
  i.e. the money drawn out was the original money and the money there at the date of insolvency was new money.
- It is of huge importance to a bank because it established the principle of 'first in, first out' i.e. the first debit out absorbs the first credit that is paid in and vice versa.
- It is of importance in many instances such as:
  - Customer's death when the account is not stopped. If overdrawn and the account carries on, then the overdrawn amount may be extinguished by any credit paid in and the bank's right over the estate could be lost
  - Ditto, with insolvency
  - When a joint account is overdrawn and one party dies, the rights against the estate of the deceased could be lost and
  - Reliance for any 'new' overdraft would have to be placed onto the survivor.

Answer 4

(a) Consider why most retail banks use several different channels. Illustrate your answer with examples. **(10 marks)**

Your answer should include the following points.

- Different channels are used because customers have different needs and banks wish to address those needs.
- They are also provided because banks wish to provide methods of delivery which are for them the most economical and some methods are much cheaper than others.
- Marks will then be awarded for the candidate's demonstration of their ability to explain at least three different methods of distribution of retail banking to customers which explain the first two bullet points (above).

RETAIL BANKING

(b) Discuss the role of people in providing some methods of delivery for bank services and why face-to-face contact can be very important in some circumstances but less so in others. Illustrate your answer with examples. **(10 marks)**

Your answer should include the following points.

- People are more important in some forms of delivery than others.

- Although people are in one way or another essential for all forms of delivery, even automated ones. In such a case though their involvement is different in that they will be filling a technical or administrative function rather than a skilled one in which they are part of the service which is being provided.

- Some customers want people to be involved in delivering their banking services, regardless of what that service is so banks have to provide some staff to do this.

- Some customers are just the opposite and specifically prefer to use automated means of access to banking services so banks provide such for these customers.

- Some services though need people to be involved. It can be difficult if not impossible to provide, for example, complex lending services without a face to face meeting. It is more or less impossible to take large cash credits without a cashier and so on.

- Answers should, after considering the general framework for the involvement or lack of people in delivering services, provide several examples to illustrate their points. Marks will be awarded for the pertinence and quality of these illustrations. **(TOTAL 20 MARKS)**

Answer 5

Explain what is meant by the term organisation. **(TOTAL 15 MARKS)**

Your answer should include the following points.

Answers should include some or all of the following factual observations:

- A social device for efficiently accomplishing through group means some stated purpose.

- Something incorporates three things, people, objectives and structure.

- People interacting with each other within the structure to achieve objectives.

- Co-ordinated activities by people for the achievement of a common goal or purpose using a division of labour and function via a hierarchy of authority and responsibility.

- Something which co-ordinates human activity to a common purpose.

Answers should always provide the basics of people, objectives and structure.

Marks to be awarded beyond these factual points in accordance with the quality of the explanation provided of how these factors work together

PRACTICE EXAMINATION 2

PRACTICE EXAM 2: QUESTIONS

Question 1

Required

(a) Explain what are the new Banking regulated authorities and the purpose of each. **(8 marks)**

(b) The PRA and PCA will to a large degree do what the FSA was supposed to have done. Explain and discuss what the largest differences in their overall approach. **(12 marks)**

(c) Describe the function of the European Banking Authority. **(10 marks)**

(TOTAL 30 MARKS)

Question 2

Required

Discuss the Consumer Credit Acts 1974 and 2006, contrasting their intent and purpose.

(TOTAL 20 MARKS)

Question 3

Required

Consider the factors which resulted in the 2007 banking crisis. Illustrate your answer with examples.

(TOTAL 15 MARKS)

Question 4

Required

(a) Explain the circumstances of the case Tournier v National Provincial and Union Bank of England Ltd. 1924. **(10 marks)**

(b) The absolute rule of secrecy owed by a bank to its customer was subsequently qualified by the listing of a series of expectations to that requirement. List when a banker can breach the duty of secretary and briefly explain in each case how this might happen. **(10 marks)**

(TOTAL 20 MARKS)

Question 5

Required

Consider why a bank ought generally to welcome complaints from customers. Your answer should use illustrations to justify your arguments. **(TOTAL 15 MARKS)**

PRACTICE EXAM 2: ANSWERS

Answer 1

(a) Explain what are the new Banking regulated authorities and the purpose of each. **(8 marks)**

Your answer should include the following points.

- The Bank of England is the overall regulating authority. To assist it three other bodies are to be set up but which will be a part of it.

- Financial Policy Committee will be the Bank's new equivalent of the current Monetary Policy Committee. It will look at the economy on a large scale basis to see issues which will effect economic and financial stability with the powers to address these issues.

- Prudential Regulatory Authority will be responsible for the regulation of retail and investment banks, building societies and insurance companies. It will ensure that they are carefully ('prudently') managed although primary responsibility for this rests with the organisations themselves.

- Financial Conduct Authority will be responsible for promoting confidence in the finance industry. It will particularly be responsible for the provision of choice and efficiency for customers, protection for customers, the integrity of the UK financial system and within its brief for the above, ensure that so far as is possible, competition is promoted.

(b) The PRA and PCA will to a large degree do what the FSA was supposed to have done. Explain and discuss what the largest differences in their overall approach. **(12 marks)**

- All marks here rest in bringing out the difference in intended approach to regulating the institutions. This is one where the 'tick box' approach will be seen less and the regulating staff's judgement of the position which they see when they review the organisations will be seen more.

- This is important because the FSA's past approach has been to have a tick list of what was required of the banks and if a tick appeared, then they were deemed to be in order without any further question.

- Majority of marks rests with how this is explained and described by the candidate.

(c) Describe the function of the European Banking Authority. **(10 marks)**

Your answer should include the following points.

- It is the Banking Regulatory Body for all European Countries.
- It is supposed to ensure common regulatory standards across the European Union.
- To protect the stability of the financial system.
- To protect the interest of consumers.
- Using a common framework that looks at the bank's funds, capital adequacy, credit, market and operational risk.
- Theoretically it can over-rule national regulators but the UK system in particular is highly resistant to this, as is the UK government. **(TOTAL 30 MARKS)**

Answer 2

Discuss the Consumer Credit Acts 1974 and 2006, contrasting their intent and purpose.

(TOTAL 20 MARKS)

Your answer should have included the following points.

- CCA 74 was introduced to protect private customers of lenders who enter into some types of consumer credit agreements.
- 2006 Act amended the 74 act to create a fairer and more competitive market.
- 74 act concerned itself with:
    - The actual contract, the agreement and its terms and conditions
    - Advertising of loans
    - APR calculation
    - Early repayment procedures
    - Default procedures
    - Extortionate credit bargains.
- All loans were included which were for less than £25,000 which were intended to be used for any consumer credit purpose.
- Exempted were agreements within families, further advances on mortgage for home renovation and improvement, loans secured on houses to buy the house (mortgages) and second mortgage borrowing.
- A consumer is an individual, an unincorporated body or a partner.
- The 2006 act took these rules after about 30 years' experience and refined them.
    - Rights and redress for consumers were made better by bringing disputes into the realm of the Financial Services Ombudsman
    - The £25,000 upper limit was removed but if the agreement is predominantly for business purposes and over £25,000 then it is outside the act
    - Judgement and fairness were introduced as measures when considering the enforcement of agreements, rather than just the wording
    - Other than individuals, only partnerships with two or three partners are caught by the act
    - High net worth individuals can be exempt from the act as borrowers or hirers if they ask for this
    - The rules relating to annual statements were tightened up
    - The rules relating to enforcement on default were made much more clear and much tighter, in the favour of the consumer
    - The concept of 'unfair relationships' was introduced which relates to loan sharks so that they could be more effectively dealt with.
- Overall, the 2006 act simply updated the 74 act and made things much more loaded in favour of borrower.
- Marks will be awarded for factual content, but about half res with the candidate's ability to discuss and demonstrate the development of the concept of consumer credit, shown by the working of the two acts.

PRACTICE EXAM 2: ANSWERS

Answer 3

Consider the factors which resulted in the 2007 banking crisis. Illustrate your answer with examples.

(TOTAL 15 MARKS)

This question is intended to allow candidates to provide an essay style answer which will enable them show their knowledge of the factual issues involved and their ability to discuss their interaction and effects. It should include some of:

- Size of the US house lending market.
- Belief that lending secured on houses was entirely safe.
- Belief that domestic property could only grow in value.
- Expansion of credit card and other consumer lending such as motor vehicle finance to the point where it was available to almost anyone for anything.
- Overheating of economies, the US and UK ones in particular.
- Problems with complex derivatives leading to serious difficulties for Goldman Sachs and Morgan Stanley, followed by Bear Sterns, Merrill Lynch and Lehman Brothers.
- The almost out of control housing lending by Fannie Mae and Freddie Mac in the US resulted in their effective demise.
- All this came as a result on one hand from an insatiable demand from the public for cheap credit with which to buy things.
- On the other its provision by lenders without much regard for how it was going to be repaid.
- Marks will be awarded for any or all of the above points (and any others of relevance) and the level of discussion and pertinent illustrations provided.

Answer 4

(a) Explain the circumstances of the case Tournier v National Provincial and Union Bank of England Ltd. 1924. **(10 marks)**

Your answer should include the following points.

- Case involved a bank manager who revealed to an employer that the customer had an overdraft and was thought to be gambling.
- Customer's three month employment contract was not renewed, he claimed as a result.
- Tournier sued bank for breach of contract.
- Bank won at first instance and appeal.
- Case is very important as it set out when a bank may breach its otherwise absolute duty of secrecy.

The more factual information and the more comment, the more marks.

(b) The absolute rule of secrecy owed by a bank to its customer was subsequently qualified by the listing of a series of expectations to that requirement. List when a banker can breach the duty of secretary and briefly explain in each case how this might happen. **(10 marks)**

Your answer should include the following points.

- Compulsion of law. Marks should be awarded here for a general explanation that if statute law requires the bank to divulge information, then the duty can be breached. Examples of the various statutes should be rewarded with marks, but not excessively so. Some examples should be provided. There are three headings and these need to be covered:
    - Compulsion of Court Order
    - When by required by statute to a suitably authorised official
    - When the initiative rests with the bank to disclose to the authority defined in statute

- Duty to the public. Here, there is no definition of what this means, but it usually taken to mean when the UK is at war with another country and an account of an alien is held by the bank. When the UK went to war with Argentina over the Falklands in 1982 for example, the Bank of England wrote to all banks seeking information about accounts of Argentinian nationals. The only guidance available from Tournier is when the duty of the bank to the nation may exceed that to the customer, which is not very helpful.

- In the interests of the Bank. Usually taken to mean when it has to justify its actions which is what happened in Tournier.

- When the customer gives express or implied consent to disclose information. This is self-explanatory, but there have been cases which have established that for example, handing over the telephone to a third party is enough to establish implied consent by the customer.

(TOTAL 20 MARKS)

Answer 5

Consider why a bank ought generally to welcome complaints from customers. Your answer should use illustrations to justify your arguments. **(TOTAL 15 MARKS)**

This question is designed to make candidates think. There are several factual issues to consider but then an argument to make which address the positive things to be gained from complaints. The factual issues should include:

- What is a complaint? Expression of dissatisfaction, resentment, grievance, cause or reason for complaining etc.
- Happens when a customer is not happy.
- Can be irrational, usually is not.
- Usually happens when something had happened that the customer does not like, or feels is unfair or makes them feel that they have been mistreated. Generally because they are not satisfied.
- If this is so, it does not really matter if the complaint is or is not justified, the customer will feel aggrieved if something is not done about it.
- Bank should welcome such because for whatever reason it has happened, the relationship is damaged because of something that the bank has or has not done.
- Bank ought either to be able to justify what it has done or conceded that it was unjustified. In either instance it is an opportunity to improve so it should be welcomed.

This question permits a high level of subjective judgement or argument to be introduced by the candidate and this is what the examiner is looking for. It might be that they show that not all complaints are to be welcomed (perhaps those about personality clashes for example) but they can all be used to learn from, however negative the customer.

Marks should be awarded for the way that the discussion is constructed and the strength of argument, which will be boosted by the power of the illustrations used.

PRACTICE EXAMINATION 3

PRACTICE EXAM 3: QUESTIONS

Question 1

Required

(a) Compare a range of distribution channels used by retail banks to reach customers. **(8 marks)**

(b) Distinguish between four different methods of money transmission showing why some might be more appropriate to some situations than others. **(12 marks)**

(c) Explain why it is important to have a range of distribution channels if a bank is to retain a range of customers. **(10 marks)**

(TOTAL 30 MARKS)

Question 2

Required

A great deal has been made of a major retail bank's decisions to remove individual sales targeting in its branches. In the context of risk in retail banking, discuss whether you think that this is a positive or negative move. **(TOTAL 20 MARKS)**

Question 3

Required

Discuss and critically appraise the argumens for and against outsourcing as they affect customer service.

(TOTAL 15 MARKS)

Question 4

Required

(a) Explain the concept of action-centred leadership. **(10 marks)**

(b) Critically appraise the concept of action-centred leadership. **(10 marks)**

(TOTAL 20 MARKS)

Question 5

Required

Explain and discuss what is meant by the term prudential control as it relates to the regulation of banks and financial services. **(TOTAL 15 MARKS)**

Answer 1

(a) Compare a range of distribution channels used by retail banks to reach customers. **(8 marks)**

Your answer should include the following points.

- A reasonable number of distribution methods need to be cited. These could include:
    - Branch banking
    - Telephone banking
    - Internet banking
    - Postal banking
- Similarly, a number of services need to be cited such as (not exclusive):
    - Money transfer
    - Obtaining and paying in cash
    - Lending
    - Statements
    - Standing orders and direct debits
    - Other bill paying
- Finally, an explanation of individual customer needs and wants needs to be provided, with an explanation of how a combination of the above should meet these. About half marks rest with the facts, the remainder with the discussion and explanation.

(b) Distinguish between four different methods of money transmission showing why some might be more appropriate to some situations than others. **(12 marks)**

As with part (a), the examiner will expect that a number of money transfer services will be cited. These could include:

- Standing orders
- Direct debits
- Cheques
- Cash
- Automated transfers via the internet
- Card based systems

The majority of marks rest not with citing the services although this is essential, but explaining why some might be more suited to some types of customer and some types of payment whilst others might not be.

(c) Explain why it is important to have a range of distribution channels if a bank is to retain a range of customers. **(10 marks)**

All that is sought here is a clear answer which shows that customers differ, how they differ and how their needs differ. We would expect that the answer will be illustrated with examples of different distribution channels and the advantages and disadvantages of their use by customers and the bank. This would include cost issues to the bank and customer. **(TOTAL 30 MARKS)**

RETAIL BANKING

Answer 2

A great deal has been made of a major retail bank's decisions to remove individual sales targeting in its branches. In the context of risk in retail banking, discuss whether you think that this is a positive or negative move. **(TOTAL 20 MARKS)**

There are not many facts to bring out here. What the examiner is looking for is:

- A recognition that if staff are targeted financially or otherwise they will respond to those targets.
- This makes it potentially risky that they will try to sell things to customers whether they need them or not.
- This puts the bank's reputation at risk.
- And potentially sets staff against each other.
- There is a danger that service levels will drop as the public perception grows that all the bank and its people are interested in is selling things whether needed or not.
- The underlying risk is that customers will leave as they become disenchanted.
- And that mis-selling could take place.
- Jobs might be deskilled in favour of a sales culture.
- Consequently staff will be less well trained to deal with the technicalities of their job rather than their ability to sell.
- We are quite happy to see a contra argument put, the marks rest entirely with the quality of the argument and its basis.

Answer 3

Discuss and critically appraise the arguments for and against outsourcing as they affect customer service. **(TOTAL 15 MARKS)**

Your answer should include the following points.

- Expertise is concentrated in one place so skill should be higher.
- But many of the outsourced jobs are routine and repetitive so skill is not high in any case.
- Consequently without the involvement of customers they may appear mundane and pointless.
- As a result, errors may actually increase.
- Customer facing staff are not able to do the task on the spot.
- So service might slow down.
- Errors and delays can be blamed on a processing centre which is likely to annoy the customer.
- Service Level agreements might address these problems but experience has been patchy.
- Other points may be raised for and against outsourcing, providing that they are valid, credit will be given.
- As with other questions, at least half the marks rest with the quality of the discussion and argument, whichever way it goes, if any, rather than the presentation of series of facts.

PRACTICE EXAM 3: ANSWERS

Answer 4

(a) Explain the concept of action-centred leadership. **(10 marks)**

Your answer should include the following points.

- Action-centred leadership involves three concentric circles, one task, one team, one individual, the area in which they all overlap is the effective part of the organisation.
- The more the overlap, the more effective the organisation.
- The task is what the organisation is there to achieve so attention must be directed towards whatever helps the team to achieve the task.
- The leader needs to look to see what can be done to bring together the team to operate as one unit to achieve the task through strong morale, motivation and a feeling of belonging.
- As teams are made of individuals, the leader must ensure so far as is practicable consistent with the other two areas, that individual needs are met, otherwise those of the team will not be met.
- For the leader to be a success, equal attention needs to be paid to each area.
- Examples should be given of how leaders may or may not do this and the likely effects.

(b) Critically appraise the concept of action-centred leadership. **(10 marks)**

(TOTAL 20 MARKS)

All the marks here lie with the discussion and argument presented, based upon part (a)'s factual content and how well, either way, the concept is critically appraised.

Answer 5

Explain and discuss what is meant by the term prudential control as it relates to the regulation of banks and financial services. **(TOTAL 15 MARKS)**

Your answer should include the following points.

- The adoption and operational awareness of the need for a balance between risk and return in running the business.
- Banking is about risk and prudential control is about controlling that risk.
- Role of adequate capital.
- Nature of capital (shares and retained profits).
- Awareness of the different activities of banks in terms of the risks that they incur.
- We expect to see some discussion of this illustrated with specific examples.
- The 'Prudential Sourcebook' from the FCA gives rules and guidelines.
- As does the Basle Agreement in terms of capital adequacy.
- The factual points above will have to be enunciated, but as ever, half the marks rest with the candidate's ability to explain and illustrate the use of the concept and issues involved.